APOSTLES of JESUS

By REV. LAWRENCE G. LOVASIK, S.V.D.

NIHIL OBSTAT: James T. O'Connor, S.T.D. *Censor Librorum*
IMPRIMATUR: ✠ James P. Mahoney, D.D., *Vicar General, Archdiocese of New York*
© 1980 by *Catholic Book Publishing Corp., N.J.* — Printed in Hong Kong
ISBN 978-0-89942-285-5

JAMES
MATTHIAS
SIMON
BARTHOLOMEW
PHILIP
THOMAS

JUDE

ANDREW   JOHN   PETER   PAUL   JAMES THE LESS   MATTHEW

SAINT PETER

SIMON Peter was a fisherman from Galilee, who was led to Jesus by his brother Andrew. "You are Simon," Jesus said. "You shall be called Peter, which means 'Rock.'"

Peter was always at Our Lord's side. Once he fished all night and caught nothing. Jesus told him to lower the net again, and he and Andrew couldn't hold all the fish they got.

Jesus told Peter: "From now on you will be fishers of men." Leaving all things, Peter and Andrew followed Jesus.

Peter's Faith in Jesus

WHEN Jesus promised the Blessed Sacrament, many of His followers left Him. He asked whether the Apostles were also going to leave.

Peter answered: "Lord, to whom shall we go? You have the words of eternal life, and we have come to believe that You are the Son of God."

One day Jesus said to Peter, "Simon, Simon! Remember that Satan has asked for you, to sift you all like wheat. But I have prayed for you that your faith may never fail. You in turn must strengthen your brothers."

"Lord," he said to Him, "at Your side I am prepared to face imprisonment and death itself."

Jesus replied, "I tell you, Peter, the cock will not crow today until you have three times denied that you know Me."

During the Passion of Our Lord, Peter denied Him out of fear for his life. But afterward he repented for what he had done.

Then after Our Lord's Resurrection, Peter spent the rest of his life telling others about Him.

Peter Walks on the Water

ONE night Jesus came walking on the water to the Apostles who were halfway across the lake. Peter asked to go to Him, and Jesus said: "Come."

Peter began to walk toward Jesus on the waves, but he soon lost courage and began to sink. He cried out: "Lord, save me." Jesus stretched out His hand and caught him.

As they got back into the boat, the wind stopped. Peter and the Apostles fell at Jesus' feet and said: "You are indeed the Son of God."

Peter the First Pope

JESUS told Peter: "You are Peter and upon this Rock I will build My Church." Peter was the first Pope of the Catholic Church.

Peter led the Church at Jerusalem, then in Antioch, and finally in Rome. He ruled kindly and worked many miracles.

In the year 67 he was crucified upside down because he considered himself unworthy to die as Jesus had. He is honored with two feasts: February 22 and June 29.

SAINT JOHN

JOHN was the youngest of the Apostles. He and his brother James had been followers of John the Baptist.

One day Jesus saw them helping their father mend fish nets. He called them: "Come, follow Me!" And from then on they stayed close to Him.

They were very devoted to Jesus and one day they wanted to call down fire on a town that refused to receive Him. He named them, "sons of thunder."

Their mother Salome asked Jesus to give them places of honor, and they pledged that they could drink of Jesus' chalice of suffering.

Jesus did not promise them places of honor, but a special share in His friendship and love. They would drink of His chalice, for they would suffer and die for the love of Jesus.

John the "Beloved Disciple"

JOHN was called the "beloved disciple," because Our Lord loved him as a special friend. He was present when Jesus raised Jairus' daughter.

On the day of the Transfiguration, John was there and was allowed to see the Divinity shine through the human body of the Savior.

At the Last Supper, John was privileged to rest his head upon the heart of Jesus. Later that night he witnessed Christ's Agony in the Garden of Olives.

John Present at the Cross

WHEN the false friend betrayed Jesus with a kiss, the true friend, John, was by His side. With Peter he followed the Master to the court of the police guard.

The courage and love of the beloved disciple drew him to the Cross at Calvary. There Jesus entrusted His Mother to John, saying: "Woman, there is your son. . . . There is your mother."

John Tells Others about Jesus

ALTHOUGH John saw Jesus die in disgrace, his love and faith were stronger than all doubts. After the Resurrection, John was the first to understand what had happened.

After the Ascension, John worked with Peter for the good of the Church. They were sent to Samaria to strengthen the believers there. Peter found a trusted companion in John.

John preached in Palestine for many years. Later he was taken prisoner to Rome. He was thrown in a pot of boiling oil, but God kept him from harm.

When he was ninety years old, he wrote his Gospel to prove that Jesus was God as well as Man.

He also wrote three letters in which he says, "Beloved, let us love one another because love is of God. God is love."

John died about the year 100 in Ephesus. His feast day is December 27.

SAINT JAMES THE GREATER

JAMES was the son of Zebedee and Salome, and the older brother of John the Evangelist. He is called "the greater" because he was called to be an Apostle before the other Apostle James.

When John the Baptist pointed out Jesus near the Jordan River, James followed his brother John to the Messiah and began his life of devotion and love.

James was with Jesus at the wedding feast of Cana. When Our Lord told the disciples that He would make them "fishers of men," James left his nets and everything else to follow Him.

When Jesus went to raise the daughter of Jairus, James went with Him together with Peter and John. He was also present at the Transfiguration and the Agony in the Garden.

James — The First Apostle to Die for Christ

JESUS called James a "son of thunder" because of his great zeal, and He promised James a share in His sufferings.

James preached the Gospel in Samaria and Judea. He also journeyed to Spain and is honored as the patron saint of that land.

James was the first Apostle to give his life for Christ. He was killed with the sword by order of King Herod Agrippa in the year 43. His feast day is July 25.

11

SAINT ANDREW

LIKE Peter his brother, Andrew was a fisherman and a follower of John the Baptist. One day he saw Jesus go by and he heard John cry: "Behold the Lamb of God."

Andrew understood that Jesus was the Messiah sent by God, and he followed Him. Turning, Jesus asked: "What are you seeking?" Andrew asked Him where He lived. And Jesus replied: "Come and see."

Andrew remained with Jesus that day. Then he went home and told Peter: "We have found the Messiah." And he led Peter to Jesus.

When Peter, and his brother Andrew, were casting a net into the sea, Jesus said to them, "Come after Me and I will make you fishers of men." They at once left their nets and became His followers.

Once when there was no food for the people, it was Andrew who found the boy with the loaves and fish that Jesus used to feed the people.

Another time, Andrew took a group of Gentiles to Jesus while He was in Jerusalem. Our Lord gave an important sermon at that time.

Andrew — The First Apostle to Hear Christ's Call

ANDREW was the first Apostle to hear Christ's call and answer it. And he brought to Jesus the one who would be the head of His Church.

After Pentecost, Andrew preached the Gospel in Greece. He was crucified on a cross in the form of the letter X in Patras, Greece, in the year 60.

His relics are kept in Constantinople and his feast day is November 30.

SAINT MATTHEW

MATTHEW, called Levi, was the son of Alphaeus. He lived at Capernaum on the Sea of Galilee.

Matthew wrote one of the four Gospels about Jesus, and in it he described his call to be an Apostle. Sitting at his desk one day, he saw Christ come to him and heard the words: "Follow Me."

At once Matthew left his work as a tax collector and followed the Master.

Matthew — The Apostle of Ethiopia

MATTHEW also told of the banquet he gave that Christ attended. People grumbled when they saw Jesus and His disciples sitting with tax collectors and sinners.

But Jesus said: "I have come not to call the just but sinners."

Matthew wrote his Gospel especially for Jewish converts before he left his own people to travel to the pagans. He wrote the words of Our Lord:

"Go and teach all nations, baptizing them in the name of the Father, and of the Son, and of the Holy Spirit. Teach them to observe all things that I have commanded you, and know that I am with you all days even to the end of the world."

Matthew is called the Apostle of Ethiopia. His shrine is at Salerno, Italy, where his relics were brought in the tenth century. His feast day is September 21.

SAINT PHILIP

PHILIP, like Peter and Andrew, was from Bethsaida. He saw John the Baptist point out Jesus as the "Lamb of God Who takes away the sin of the world," and he decided to follow Him.

He sought out his friend Nathaniel and told him about the Master: "We have found the One about Whom Moses and the Prophets wrote— Jesus of Nazareth."

Nathaniel asked: "Can any good come out of Nazareth?" Philip replied: "Come and see!" Then both followed Our Lord.

It was to Philip that Jesus turned before multiplying the loaves in the desert, asking him where they could buy bread for the crowds.

Philip answered: "Thirty dollars' worth of bread would not be enough for them even if everyone would take only a little."

Philip — Crucified for Christ

A T THE Last Supper, it was Philip who said to Jesus: "Lord, show us the Father and it is enough for us."

Jesus replied: "Whoever sees Me sees the Father." Then He added: "If any man loves Me, he will keep My word, and My Father will love him. And We will come to him, and make Our dwelling with him."

After Pentecost, Philip preached the Gospel in Asia Minor. He was crucified at Hieropolis in Phrygia in the year 80. His feast day is May 3.

SAINT BARTHOLOMEW

BARTHOLOMEW means "son of Tolmai." He lived near Bethsaida and was also known as Nathaniel. He was brought to Jesus by his friend Philip.

When Jesus saw the two friends coming to Him, He spoke to Nathaniel: "Behold an Israelite indeed in whom there is no evil."

Nathaniel wondered how Jesus knew his name. But Jesus said: "Before Philip called you, when you were under the fig tree, I saw you."

At once Nathaniel made this act of faith: "Master, You are the Son of God. You are the King of Israel."

Nathaniel was present when Jesus showed Himself after His Resurrection to several of His followers on the lake shore.

Bartholomew — Preached the Gospel in Armenia

AFTER the Ascension, Bartholomew preached the Gospel in Arabia and northwest India as well as in Asia Minor. He suffered martyrdom in Armenia. His skin was cut from his living body.

This holy Apostle's relics are in the Church of Saint Bartholomew at Rome. His feast day is August 24.

19

SAINT THOMAS

THOMAS was called Didymus, which means "the twin." When Jesus decided to risk his life to visit His friend Lazarus, Thomas cried: "Let us also go, that we may die with Him."

It was also Thomas who at the Last Supper asked the question that received the beautiful answer of Our Lord: "I am the Way, and the Truth, and the Life."

After the Resurrection, the Apostles said to Thomas: "We have seen the Lord." But he said: "Unless I see in His hands the print of the nails, and put my finger into the place of the nails, and put my hand into His side, I will not believe."

Eight days later, Thomas was with the Apostles. Jesus came, the door being shut, and stood before Thomas and said: "Bring here your finger, and see My hands; and bring here your hand, and put it into My side. And be not unbelieving but believing."

Thomas Professes His Faith in Jesus

THOMAS answered; "My Lord and my God!" And Jesus said to him: "Because you have seen Me, Thomas, you have believed. Blessed are they who have not seen, and yet have believed."

After the Ascension, Thomas preached the Gospel in Parthia. He is also called the Apostle of the Indies, where he was martyred. His feast day is July 3.

SAINT JAMES

JAMES was a cousin of Our Lord and a brother of the Apostle Jude. He is known as James "the Less" because he was called to be an Apostle after the other James.

James received one of the first visions of the Risen Savior. He was appointed Bishop of Jerusalem by Our Lord Himself. He was highly respected by Jews and Gentiles alike.

James wrote a letter that shows him to be a man of calm mind and trust in Jesus, a man of prayer and devotion to the poor.

He writes: "My brothers, what good is it to profess faith without practicing it? Such faith has no power to save one, has it? Be assured, then, that faith without works is as dead as a body without breath."

He was called "the Just" because of his great love for prayer. It is said that he prayed so much that his knees became as hard as those of a camel. He drank no wine and ate no animal food.

James — A Martyr for Christ

DURING the persecution in the year 42, James remained as the Bishop of Jerusalem. After twenty years of labor for the Kingdom of God, at the age of eighty-six he was flung from the top of a tower for honoring Christ as the Son of God.

His relics are kept in Rome with those of his fellow-Apostle, Saint Philip, with whom he is honored on May 3.

SAINT SIMON THE ZEALOT

SIMON is called "the Zealot" or "the Cananean" because he was a member of a group known as the Zealots. Their aim was to keep aflame the patriotic spirit of the Jews.

Simon is one of the so-called "brethren of the Lord," that is, cousins of Jesus. He is the brother of James the Less and Jude (who were Apostles) and Joseph (who was not).

Simon's father was Alphaeus or Cleophas. His mother was Mary, a sister-in-law of the Blessed Virgin Mary.

At the Last Supper, Jesus said sadly: "Let us go to meet the traitor." Simon burst out with the words: "Lord, here are two swords." He was willing to defend his Master even at the risk of his life.

Simon — Apostle of Arabia

AFTER the coming of the Holy Spirit, Simon preached the Gospel in Arabia with Jude.

When they refused to adore false gods, they were put to death for their faith in Jesus Christ, the Son of God.

Simon was sawed in half and Jude was beheaded in Persia about the end of the first century. Their feast day is October 28.

SAINT JUDE THADDEUS

JUDE Thaddeus was a nephew of Mary and Joseph, and a cousin of Our Lord. He was a brother of the Apostles James the Less and Simon.

His father was Cleophas, who died a martyr, and his mother's name was Mary. She stood beneath the Cross when Jesus died, and later came to anoint His body.

Some of the Apostles were looking for the founding of an earthly kingdom. So even at the Last Supper Jude asked Jesus: "Lord, how is it that You will show Yourself to us and not to the world?"

However, after the coming of the Holy Spirit, Jude and his fellow-Apostles at last understood what Jesus meant when He said that His Kingdom was to be in this world but not of the world.

Jude begins his Epistle with the words: "Jude, a servant of Jesus Christ and brother of James, to those who have been called by God; who have found love in God the Father and have been guarded safely in Jesus Christ."

Jude — Patron of Impossible Cases

JUDE preached the Gospel in Arabia together with Simon. They were killed for their faith about the year 100.

Jude was beaten to death with a club and then beheaded. His relics are in Rome. He is very popular as the patron of impossible cases. His feastday is October 28.

SAINT MATTHIAS

THE early Christian preachers were all Jews, and the world of that day hated Jews. They were also all Galileans (except for Paul and Judas), and so even the rest of the Jews hated them.

Our Lord chose the weak things to overcome the strong—the Greek and Roman world of that day. God used twelve ignorant fishermen to spread His religion throughout the world.

They were successful because the Holy Spirit helped them. He spoke in and through them.

Matthias was one of the first disciples of Jesus, and had been with Him from the time of Jesus' Baptism by John in the Jordan until His last days in Jerusalem.

Matthias — Apostle of Ethiopia

AFTER the Ascension of Our Lord, Peter proposed that the disciples draw lots to choose an Apostle to take the place of Judas. The Holy Spirit guided them to choose Matthias.

Matthias preached the Gospel in Judea and afterward in Ethiopia. He was stoned to death in the year 64. His feastday is May 14.

SAINT PAUL

PAUL was a Jew who hated the Christians. He was on his way to arrest them when a light from heaven suddenly shone around him.

Saul fell to the ground and heard the words: "Saul, Saul, why do you persecute Me?" He asked: "Who are You, Lord?"

The voice replied: "I am Jesus, Whom you are persecuting." Saul asked: "Lord, what do You want me to do?" The voice told him to go into the city and he would be told.

Paul — Apostle of the Gentiles

PAUL had to be led by his companions, for he had been struck blind. After three days a man named Ananias came to him and said: "Brother Saul, the Lord has sent me—Jesus Who appeared to you—that you may get back your sight and be filled with the Holy Spirit."

At once Saul could see. He was baptized and called Paul. He began to preach the word of Jesus to the pagan world.

Paul was a tent maker. He supported himself by his trade even when he was preaching the Gospel of Jesus. He is called the Apostle of the Gentiles, though he was not one of the first twelve apostles.

He begins his letter to the Colossians with the words: "Paul, an apostle of Christ Jesus by the will of God. May God our Father give you grace and peace."

Paul was a great preacher, theologian, organizer, writer, and missionary. He wrote many Epistles to the Churches he founded on his missionary journeys.

Paul Preaches to the Greeks

PAUL would willingly speak of Jesus to anyone that would listen. He even preached at the world-renowned Areopagus of Greece. And he made a few converts of the philosophers there.

In Rome in the ·year 67, Paul gained the crown of martyrdom. He was beheaded outside the walls of Rome on the Ostian Way.

His remains are in Saint Paul's Basilica at Rome and he is honored on two feast days: January 25 and June 29.